MW00723513

# Sugary Boogery Book

*A Healthy Dose of Sweet and Gross*

by Kris Beckman
Illustrated by Allison Baty and Kris Beckman

Copyright © 2015 Kris Beckman
All rights reserved.

ISBN: 0692272992
ISBN 13: 9780692272992
Library of Congress Control Number: 2014916400
Kris Beckman
Kansas City MO

For Kate and Carson

I'll give you a million cookies and hugs
And hope for no sugar booger bugs
Please remember to brush
And always flush

# Sugary Boogery Book

It's a healthy dose of sweet and gross
A bit of a teasable tongue twister
Like baby talk from baby sister
The poems are ooey gooey
Sticky and tricky
Some boogery
Some sugary
Some happy
Some sappy
There's some that make you laugh
And some that will make grandma gasp
Enjoy the book and the pictures too
All were created just for you

# ONE MAN WRECKING MACHINE

I have a one man wrecking machine
She's anything but clean
She opens doors
Pulls out drawers
Saves trash
Makes a splash
Forgets to flush
Walks in slush
Has stuff laying around
Waiting to be found
Like wrappers from candy
Shoes that are sandy
Hair bows
Dirty clothes
Yesterday's snack
Her school backpack
All on the floor
With an apple core
Little notes
Toy boats
Stickers galore
I can take no more
The only thing worse would be
A two man wrecking machine and me

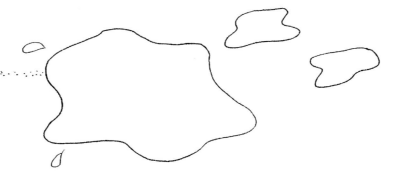

## BEAR HUNT

Going on a bear hunt and I'm
   going to bring
All sorts of interesting things
A flashlight
Dynamite
Two pails
One inch nails
My sleeping bag
A U.S. flag
A snack or two
Irish stew
A tent for sleep
An Easter Peep
A needle and thread
A blow up bed
A warm coat
A gravy boat
My Big Cedar map
My big bear trap
Some toilet paper
A tiny ice scraper

A cardboard box
My collection of rocks
Some candy for sure
A fishing lure
My favorite book
Some gobbledegook
A boo boo patch
A very dry match
A teddy bear
A comb for hair
Dental floss
BBQ sauce
A grill
And a drill
A hat
And a bat
A doll
And a ball
I think that's all
This hunt's gonna be fun
Hope I find just one

## LET IT BEE

My mom says, "If I leave it be
It won't sting me!"
But if playing in clover
It's all over
Buzzzzzzzzzzz
"Ouch!" I cry
"Why? Why? Why?"

## SNIPE HUNT

I had never heard of a snipe
What was all the hype?
How hard can it be
To hunt a thingy?
You will never know
Until you go
On a snipe hunt

## OUR UGLY TOES

A mutual reveal
That was the deal
Sitting side by side
With something to hide
We agreed to disclose
Our ugly toes
On the count of three
Feet be free
Mine is a bunion
Like the bulb of an onion
On the side of my foot
Sprouting out like a root
It gets sore and red
My little bunion head
But what about him
And his lower limb?
A hammer toe
It can't be so
It isn't right
It's pulled so tight
It's not something I seek
But it's unique
Toes embraced
Hearts raced
It's hard to think of
That feet fell in love

## MIXED VEGGIE WEDGIES

One day I asked my mom what a wedgie was
I needed to know...just because
She looked at me and then at dad
She seemed confused and a little sad
She let out a sigh
And told a lie
She said it's when food gets underneath
And caught between your teeth
After dinner that night mom read me a book
I say, "Whoa!  You should go look...
You've got two wedgies
Of mixed veggies!"

## GOTTA GO

The other night I was lying in bed
Thoughts of pee in my head
I tossed and turned
Unconcerned
Because I had just went
My bladder's content
I tossed and turned a little while longer
Thoughts of pee getting stronger
To the bathroom I decided to go
"Ouch!" I stubbed my little toe
Despite the delay
I found my way
To that dark, cold spot
The porcelain pot
My eyes were so very sleepy
No longer gotta pee pee
"Dog gone it!" I shout
Toilet paper is out!

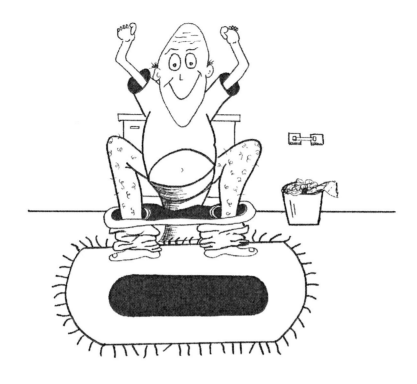

## WHERE IS PAPA?

I forgot
Papa's on the pot
A big surprise
For my eyes
A state of shock
I couldn't talk
There he was
Doing what he does
Things decompose
Help!  My nose!

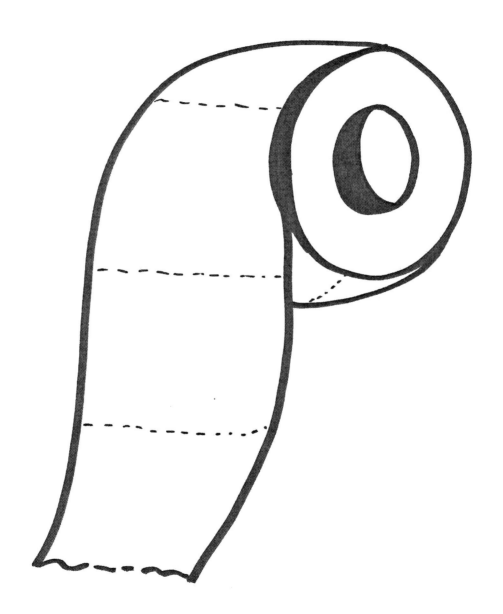

# BATHROOM WORDS

My mom says you can only use these words in one room
It's the room where we groom
Where we do our duty
Where we wipe our bootie
So here I sit
On the toilet
Saying the words aloud
My mom would be proud
Poop poop poop
All in a group
Kids at the pool
I learned that at school
Tinkle tinkle tinkle
Another word for sprinkle
Number 2
PEW!
Hershey squirt
I bet that hurt
Super-size
Cow pies
One big fart
It's off the chart
Excuse me
While I pee
Privacy please
I have to squeeze
After all this, I'm none the wiser
But I make good fertilizer

# MAGIC IN A BAR

Soap is magic
What otherwise could be tragic
It removes the grime
Works every time
Takes away silly tattoos
And sticky glue
It really erases
And leaves no traces
It removes markers that won't fade
Ones that come in every shade
Grass stained knees
And yummy nacho cheese
It's the "Dirt Police"
Takes away stubborn grease
Good-bye stamps on my arm
Works like a charm
Good-bye drawings on my feet
Soap will just delete
It's magic in a bar
Somewhat bizarre
Soap removes the obscene
So I can be clean

## FACE CLEANER

My mom invades my space
When she licks her finger
And cleans my face!

## MOMMIES ARE THE BEST

Us Mommies are often put to the test
Though we try our very best
It's so nice when they rest
Or when they get themselves ready and dressed
But too often we feel stressed
Because the house is a mess
Laundry isn't put away in the chest
We forgot to thaw the chicken breast
The cat is acting all depressed
And to make it worse we have an unwelcome guest
Lice, that is, …what a pest
I'm sure I won't go into cardiac arrest
But I'm totally unimpressed
Timmy thinks he's from the wild wild west
Screaming "Hands up, you're under arrest"
His little sister is acting possessed
Climbing up my favorite dress
Just when I think there's nothing left
Patches must be sewn on the vest
But then I remember I am very blessed
To have these little ones in my nest
Even with all the requests
Being a mom is the best!

# I LOVE YOU

I love you so
I want you to know
Your big brown eyes
Your questions why
Your mustache lips
Your helpful tips
Your dancing
Your prancing
Your heart
Your art
Your singing, listen, I hear it
And most of all your giving spirit
I love you so
I want you to know
When happy or sad
When good or bad
When it's unclear
You're always near
In my heart
We're never apart

# I LOVE MY MOM

I'm attached to my mom
My hand in her palm
I hang on her arm
I mean no harm
Wiping hands on her dress
Laying on her chest
I'm like a little fawn
To simply love on
Or a baby kangaroo
Stuck like glue
Climbing her is fun
Though I weigh a ton
I'm taking her over
Like a weed in clover
I need her special touch
It's all because I love my mom so much

## MY CHESTER RACCOON

This day's come too soon
For my Chester Raccoon
Tomorrow's her first day
When I send her away
And when I'm feeling weak
I'll press my hand to my cheek

A kiss just for you
My boogaboo
My honey pooh
My smoocharoo
I love you!

## ALWAYS THERE

It's something you wear
And it's always there
You can't wipe them away
Guaranteed to stay
No matter how hard you try
You can't say good-bye
What is this?
A mother's kiss

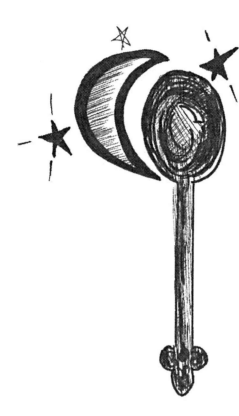

## SPOON

When there's a moon
My parents spoon
Warm and snug
A vertical hug
I think they're gross
A little too close

# AWAKE

I can't sleep
Not a peep
Tried all sides
Eyes wide
Tossed and turned
Tummy churned
Tick tock tick tock
It's 3 o'clock
Counted sheep
Still no sleep
Feeling cozy
Still no dozy
Sun's not out
I want to shout
Must be still
Sleeping pill?
Tick tock tick tock
It's 4 o'clock
Moon is shining

I'm still whining
Counted frogs
To saw some logs
No such luck
I feel stuck
Wide awake
How 'bout a break?
Tick tock tick tock
It's 5 o'clock
It's still dark
I need to park
My tired head
On my bed
At last I rest
What a quest
My eyes close
I start to doze
Off to sleep...

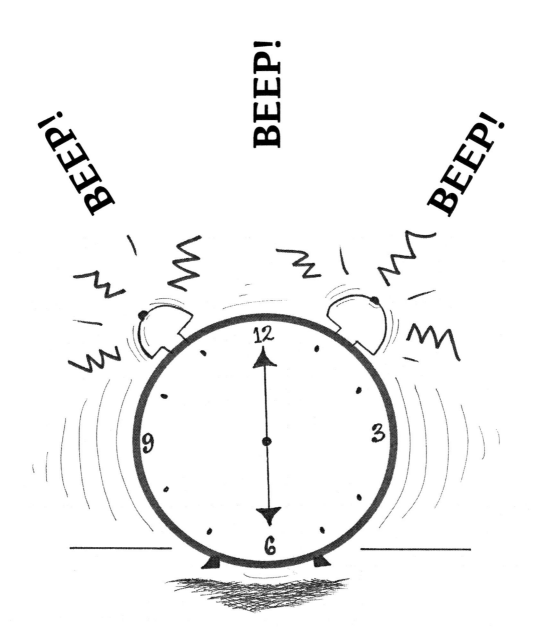

# WIRED

But, but, but... I'm not tired
I'm just wired
I've eaten candy
Isn't that dandy?
I drank a pop
Watch me flop
On my belly
Jiggles like jelly
Makes me giggle
As I wiggle
I know how to shake
Like a snake
Up I climb
I juggle limes
Up the stairs
Let's do hair
Jump up, jump down
Twirl twirl twirl around
Stand on my head
Jump on the bed
Watch me
I'm flying free
Let's do a dance
Called "Pony Prance"
Spin me
Whoppppeeeee!
Dress-up
Giddy-up
"More!" I say
I want to play
I'm not tired
I'm just wired

## COLLECTION

I have a special wall
A space that's small
It's right by my bed
Where I lay my head
I'm the only one that knows
A secret, I suppose
This wall has a big selection
Of my booger collection

## SILENCE

Hear that? Neither do I
No baby cry
No questions why
Sigh... shut eye!

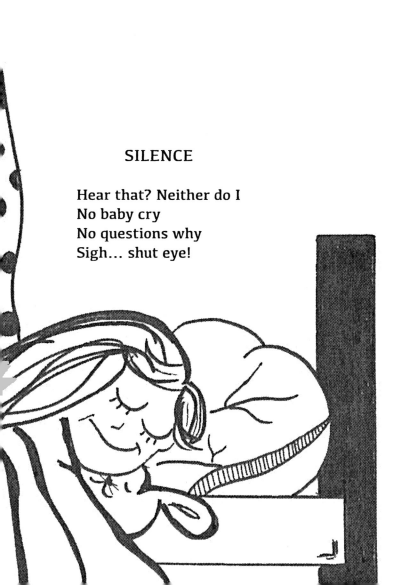

# NIGHT TIME COVER THIEF

I hope no one discovers
I'm stealing the covers
I don't make a sound
Hoping not to be found
I get cold at night
So I snuggle up tight
With my mom and dad
Is that so bad?

## BIRTHDAY SUIT

My birthday suit
It's really cute
I still can't believe it fit
When I was born in it
And I can wear it today
What can I say?
My Birthday suit
It's oh so cute!

# BOSSY ROSSY

Bossy Rossy was mean
He owned a trampoline
Bossy Rossy didn't like to share
But if he did you better beware
He would tell you how and when to jump

"Head up, don't slump!"

"Higher!" he would say

"You have to do it my way!"

"I want you to flip

and do a dip!"

"Now jump to the right

I haven't got all night!"

Bossy Rossy's not nice
He's cold as ice
Friends stopped coming over to play
They'd rather eat a worm buffet
So Bossy Rossy ended up alone
Unwilling to leave his mighty throne
And in the end he felt nothing but loss
Because he wanted to be a boss

## PROBLEM SOLVER

Problem solver, that's me
Listen up and you'll agree
Molly made me cry
I punched her in the eye
Jane wouldn't share
I pulled her curly hair
Mommy made me mad
I told Dad
Finding a solution is key
Problem solver, that's me!

# BULLY BILL

Bully Bill
Is destined to kill
He's seventeen
And really mean
Picks on me
And Natalie
No reason why
He makes us cry
He should shut his lid
Not pick on kids
He will grow up one day
And have to pay
He will be in jail
Without any bail
That's the way it is
If a bully is your biz

# RED

I'd rather be dead
Than red on the head
These words I spoke
It was a joke
About a girl I knew not well
Her last name... Mitchell
Knowing what I do now
That hair...wow!
Rich, thick and curly
Beautiful and girly
A mane that I could braid
The absolute perfect shade
A fiery hint
Of her intent
To do good
To be understood
I bet she's smart
Owns art
Tries to be green
Has substantial means
I bet she has success
And knows how to dress
Red on the head
I think I misread

# EMPTY

I have a friend named Empty
He's never full
And kind of dull
Maybe because he's empty

# NO USE

I'm running on an empty tank
Nothing's left in my bank
I'm out of gas
I might collapse
My battery's low
I'm rather slow
I'm out of juice
I'm no use
Dead man walking
No more talking

## MERMAID SISTER

Dad says it will never be
A little sister for sweet sweet me
So I made one up in my mind
She's beautiful and kind
Water is her pleasure
She knows where there's treasure
She has a pet sea horse
She's a mermaid, of course
I could have a mermaid making debut
It wouldn't be that hard to do
I would close my eyes and make a wish
But I'm scared dad might think she's a fish
And catch her with his fishing pole
And grill her over some fiery coal
So I'll just keep my mermaid sister in my head
Better there than cooked and dead

## LEMONADE STAND

It's at the corner of Main and Grand
My lemonade stand
Enjoy the shade
And some lemonade
Invite your friends to join
And bring a coin
A nickel will do
A penny too
I hope you come to my lemonade stand
See you at the corner of Main and Grand

# ELFIS

My elf lands in funny places
Never leaving any traces
I can't predict where he will be
Sometimes in our Christmas tree
He's been known to cross the line
Playing in things that are clearly mine
A whisker-free face was his dream
We caught him with dad's shaving cream
You never know
Where he will show
The coffee pot
The mail slot
Barbie's car
The jelly jar
The freezer door
Mom's dresser drawer
My Christmas stocking
That was shocking!
He's making sure that I obey
Showing me the proper way
He's a rather mischievous elf

Seems like he should worry 'bout
himself
He's always on the move
Places I don't approve
Hangs from the chandelier
Rides on my reindeer
One day he had a close call
He took a bad fall
He lay there for hours
No sign of elf powers
But the next day
He was at play
Back from the North Pole
On the toilet bowl
I have a feeling he says nice things
about me
To his boss... Mr. C.
It's not like he has room to talk
I'm not worried, I still squawk
Until he makes a change for the best
I remain unimpressed

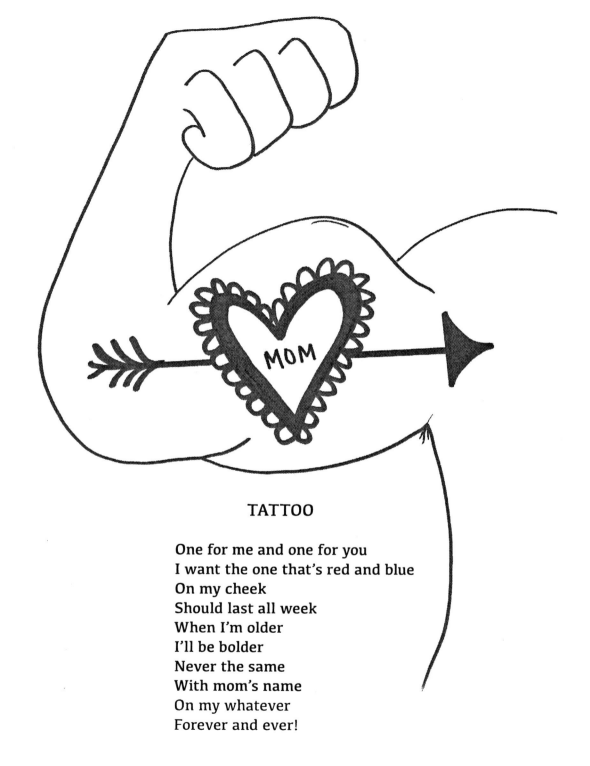

## TATTOO

One for me and one for you
I want the one that's red and blue
On my cheek
Should last all week
When I'm older
I'll be bolder
Never the same
With mom's name
On my whatever
Forever and ever!

## ARM PITS

We all have them
Including him
Kids too
Me and you
Arm pits
Yes, that's it!
Arm pits
That's funny wits
Tickle, Tickle
Smells like pickle
Some are stinky
Some are dinky
Some are wet
Because of sweat
Some have hair
Some are bare
We all have pits
I guess that's it

# MILK FOUNTAIN

A mountain of bubbles
It doubles and doubles
Made with milk and a straw
And that's about all
Deep breath and blow
Bubbles will flow
A milk fountain is fun
So go make one

## LUNCHBOX THIEF

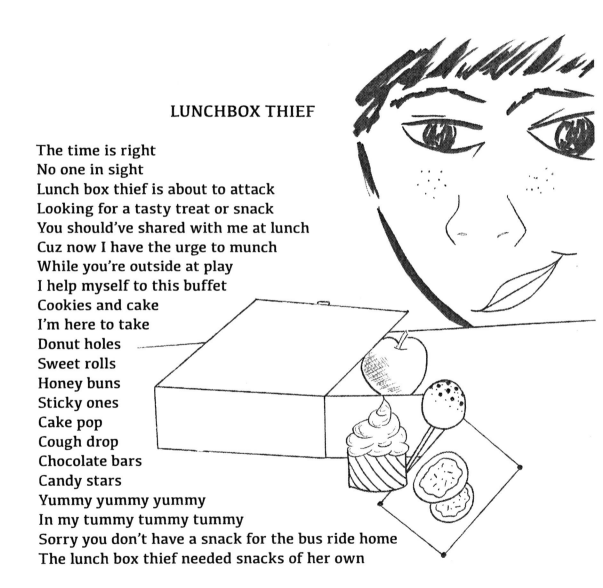

The time is right
No one in sight
Lunch box thief is about to attack
Looking for a tasty treat or snack
You should've shared with me at lunch
Cuz now I have the urge to munch
While you're outside at play
I help myself to this buffet
Cookies and cake
I'm here to take
Donut holes
Sweet rolls
Honey buns
Sticky ones
Cake pop
Cough drop
Chocolate bars
Candy stars
Yummy yummy yummy
In my tummy tummy tummy
Sorry you don't have a snack for the bus ride home
The lunch box thief needed snacks of her own

POP UP

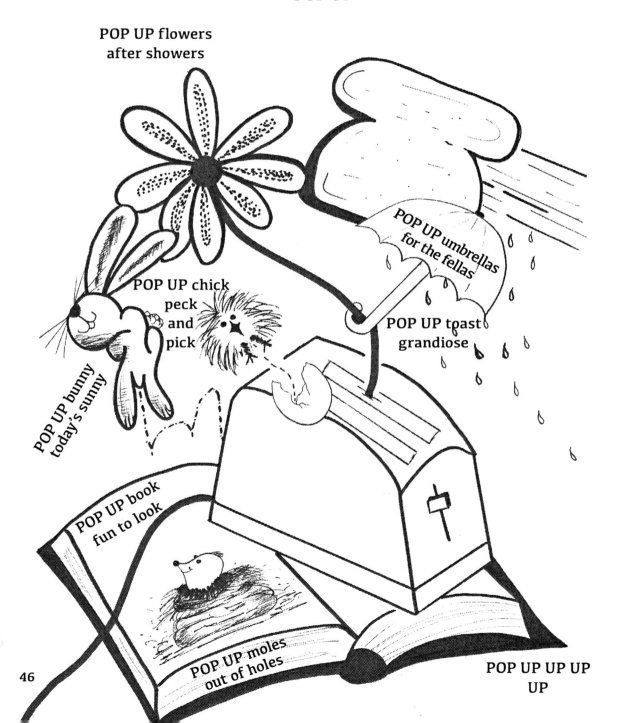

POP UP flowers
after showers

POP UP umbrellas
for the fellas

POP UP chick
peck
and
pick

POP UP toast
grandiose

POP UP bunny
today's sunny

POP UP book
fun to look

POP UP moles
out of holes

POP UP UP UP
UP

# CARTOONS

Dora the Explorer drives me nuts
Monkey Boots is such a klutz
I'm not a fan of that fox named Swiper
Does he wear a baby's diaper?
And what about that show with rabbits?
They try so hard to teach good habits
It has a bunny named Max
And sister Ruby - please relax!
"Oso"... I never met someone with such a name
Maybe that's why he has no fame
Palm pilots were out decades ago
Say bye-bye to your show
I'm uncertain about the clubhouse
You know, the home of that famous mouse
I'm mostly puzzled with that boy named Pete
He needs to eat one less sweet
And why do these toons have only four fingers?
And why are they all such terrible singers?
I'm slightly annoyed with things cartoon
Maybe because I've been watching since noon!

# SPRING BREAK

It's spring break
What will we take?
A pair of boots
A cute swimsuit
Cozy slippers
Fingernail clippers
A hair dryer
Fancy attire
Make-up
A coffee cup
An alarm clock
Shoes and socks
A fishing net
I think I'm set
But where will we go?
I don't know
To the zoo
Or maybe Peru
How about the shore
Or El Salvador
The San Francisco Bay
A park to play
A baseball game
The Hall of Fame
The grand White House
Or the home of Mickey Mouse
A video arcade
A big parade

What will we see?
A money tree
A black bear
Famous Cher
Schools of sharks
Firework sparks
Desert soil
Fields of oil
Works of art
A mini-mart
A Broadway show
Lots of snow
Beautiful mountains
Kansas City fountains
How'll we get there?
A cab fare
By ship
Zippity zip
By car
We'll go far
By plane
Or in a train
Hitchhike
Ride a bike
Go by bus
Call Gus
Subway, Segway
Let's leave today

## WHERE AM I?

It's dry
And high
Go on a hike
Or use a bike
Little green
Is ever seen
Lots of heat
Nothing to eat
It's not flat
Where am I at?
Take a guess
There's just one
's'

49

# HOMEWORK

Homework really really stinks
That's what my brain really thinks
It's on overload
It might explode
My head's full and muddy
Because it's got to study
Writing, reading, and research
I'd much rather be in church

## PERFECT STUDY BUDDY

I need a study buddy
Who's not a fuddy duddy
Whose brain's not muddy
Or like silly putty

# GETTING DRESSED

Sometimes mom gets stressed
When getting me dressed
It's always a rush
Can't find the brush
My shoes disappeared
My head feels weird
What to wear?
I *do* care
A princess gown
My mom frowns
I choose high heels
"Never!" she squeals
We decide on a skirt
Disagree on a shirt
None seem to fit
Or holes in it
We compromise

A shirt my size
We need socks that match
Ones that don't scratch
We decide on a pair
But now we do hair
She pulls and twists
I make a fist
She threatens to cut it short
Cuz I'm not a good sport
We are almost done
We've got to run
But my toothbrush is misplaced
And we're out of toothpaste
A quick water rinse
It makes her wince
A hug, a kiss, and an I love you
See you later, when school is through

## CLIP AND SNIP

I'm tired of dolls
And playing with balls
Let's do hair
Mom won't care
We will wash and style
This may be awhile
I need scissors that cut
Keep your eyes shut
Snip Snip Snip
Clip Clip Clip
Hmmmmm, not quite straight
Hmmmmm, just wait
Snip Snip Snip
Clip Clip Clip
Not Looking too good
You need a hood

# GARBAGE CAN MAN

Here I lay in the garbage can
With all gross things known to man
A take out box
Grandpa's sock
Toe nail clippings
Bacon grease drippings
Candy wrappers
Mouse trappers
Stinky diaper traces
My old shoe laces
A dried up pear
Dad's nose hair
Mice droppings
Pizza toppings
Vinaigrette
A cigarette
Fish bones
Lots of unknowns…
In the garbage can

# TALK TALK TALKER

Who is this guy?
He's never shy
Talk Talk Talk
It's eight o'clock
There's nothing he can't talk about
Weather and the summer drought
Talk Talk Talk
It's nine o'clock
I'm learning so much
Ancestors are Dutch
Talk Talk Talk
It's ten o'clock
This really is some interesting stuff
Empty boxes, oddly enough
Talk Talk Talk
It's eleven o'clock
The Stock exchange
Rare pocket change
Talk Talk Talk
It's twelve o'clock
Is there such thing as talker's block?

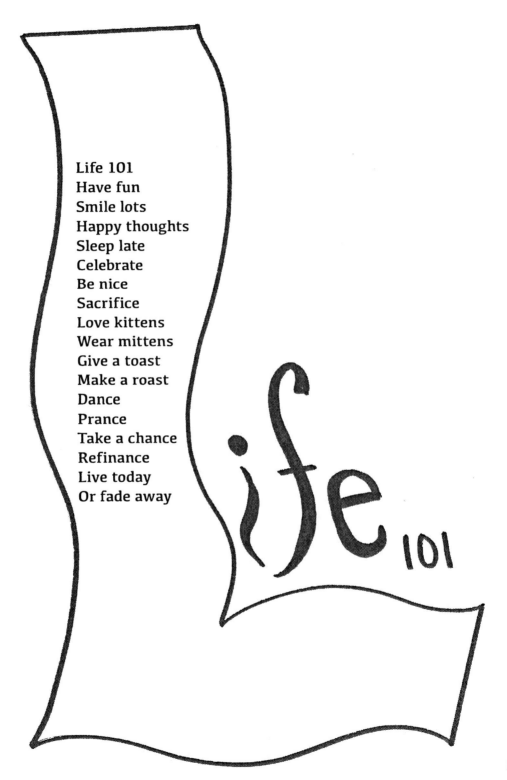

Life 101
Have fun
Smile lots
Happy thoughts
Sleep late
Celebrate
Be nice
Sacrifice
Love kittens
Wear mittens
Give a toast
Make a roast
Dance
Prance
Take a chance
Refinance
Live today
Or fade away

# TRUE LOVE

Things are not blurred
At 8944 West 63rd
A husband and wife
A simple life
Sacrifices were made
Prayers were prayed
He went off to war
She loved him more
She's his strength and his light
She's a beautiful sight
He knows her heart
They're never apart
The love they share
Is all too rare

# GREAT GRANDPA

Grandpa Kollar was great
Always early, never late
He had a heart of gold
Lots of stories he told
He was very wise
Up before the sun would rise
He wore a John Deere cap
Loved an afternoon nap
He would drive his pick-up
And sip coffee from his cup
He made CB calls
And wore Key overalls
With dirty work boots
And chewing Juicy Fruits
He would work past dark
He was a card playing shark
He deeply loved his wife
And appreciated life

## NEST

It was one of a kind
Perfectly designed
Leaves and hair
Sewn with care
A sprig and a twig
It's not very big
Ribbon and string
Almost anything
Nature's best
A beautiful nest


## GRANDMA

My grandma's the best
She's like a treasure chest
She can drive boats
Cure sore throats
She's never mean
And really clean
She lets me cook
And reads me books
Calms my worries
And tells me stories
Throws parties with themes
That make me beam
When it's time to rest my head
Animals are waiting on my bed
Grandma is the best
My favorite jewel in my treasure chest

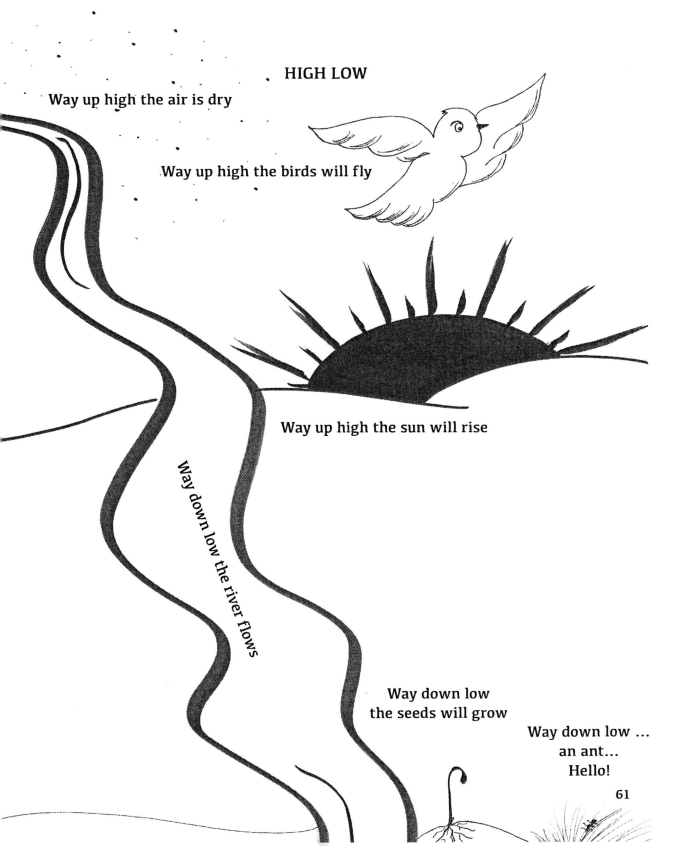

# HIGH LOW

Way up high the air is dry

Way up high the birds will fly

Way up high the sun will rise

Way down low the river flows

Way down low
the seeds will grow

Way down low ...
an ant...
Hello!

61

# BUSY BUS

There's ten of us
That ride the Busy Bus
We get on everyday
To work, shop and play
There's Carson, Drew, Betty and Pam
Carrie, Paul, Sue, Kate, and Sam

Run Carson run!
You're stop number one
You're a little late
Busy Bus won't wait

Here's stop number two
And we're picking up Drew
He's a hard working man
With a really good tan

Who will it be
At stop number three?
It is that girl Betty
Who loves spaghetti

We are picking up one more
At stop number four
Her name is Pam
She has a pet lamb

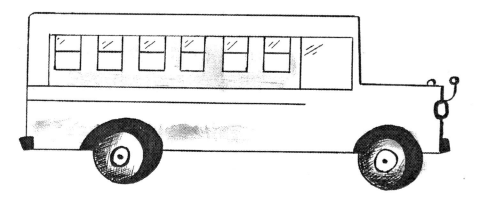

It is quite a drive
To stop number five
We pick up Carrie
Who lives on the prairie

Stop six is our friend Paul
Who frequents the shopping mall
He has lots of charm
And only one arm

Stop seven is Sue's
She has heart tattoos
She plays the drums
And chews bubblegum

We made it to stop eight
Good morning Miss Kate
She sings when we pick her up
And drinks milk from a sippy cup

Right on time
Stop number nine
It's Sam, the architect
A person we all respect

On to stop ten
It's almost the end
Who will it be?
Why, it's me

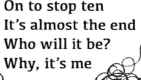

63

# FATHER BRUCE

To a wonderful man
Who followed God's plan
He led many people
At St E's steeple
Glowing with spirit
You could almost hear it
Always a smile
Always worthwhile
Engaged eyes
Very wise
Heart-felt talks
And silly socks
A beautiful voice
Let's rejoice
Kids eager to sit at the end of the pew
Waiting for a bonk by you know who
Always spreading love
Sent from above
Peace you leave
Peace we receive
Father Bruce, we celebrate you
And all that you do

# MISS ERIN AND MISS KAY

It's no bed of roses
Wiping running noses
But they love everyone
And I think they're fun!
We have a gerbil named Rosie
Our room's really cozy
We make a mess
And love recess
We have a daily routine
A well oiled machine
Jobs are split
Snack's a hit
Tables and chairs
Help with prayer
I like caboose
And Father Bruce
Our room has toys
Noise
Joys and
Boys
It has books
And hooks
Clocks
And blocks
I love making art
I always feel smart
I feel secure
And I know for sure
It's because of you
I made it through
Pre-K's the best
I feel blessed!

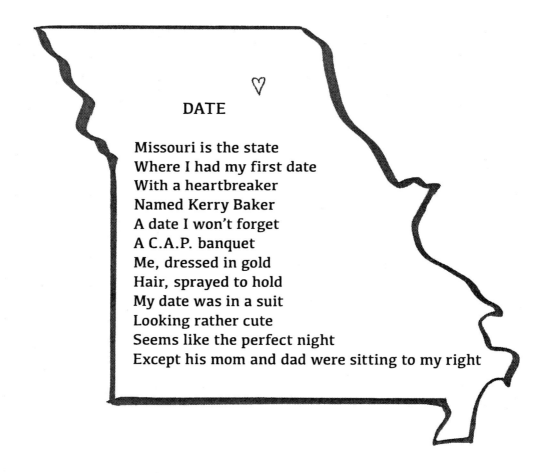

### DATE

Missouri is the state
Where I had my first date
With a heartbreaker
Named Kerry Baker
A date I won't forget
A C.A.P. banquet
Me, dressed in gold
Hair, sprayed to hold
My date was in a suit
Looking rather cute
Seems like the perfect night
Except his mom and dad were sitting to my right

## FOOTSTEPS

Shoes shoes shoes
Lots to choose
It was a store
Shoes and more
Boots of all kinds
Lots of good finds
Great Deals
On high heals
Bright colored flats
Fancy Straw hats
High tops
Flip flops
Calico
Durango
Kangaroos
To name a few
Shoe repair
Downtown square
Kirksville was the city
Pretty itty bitty
It was fun while it last
A thing of the past

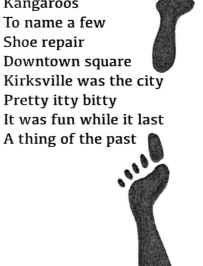

# GROWING UP KIRKSVILLE

I've been told
I'm getting old
And I guess it's true
When you look at the new
There's no more Golden Spike
There's no more Mike the Bike
No more Kaleidoscope
No more ski slope
Easter's Grocery store
It is no more
And the missing link?
Leo's Roller Rink
And the downtown has definitely changed
It's all been neatly rearranged
And why oh why
Did they say good-bye?
Troester's and Mr. Jim's
Who's fixing hems?
And what if I need a long john?
Doughboy Donuts ... they're gone!

And all the great places to eat
Like Deli Works on Franklin Street
There were so many fabulous stores
And the place where I first saw Star Wars
Kennedy Theatre it was
So fun and all the buzz!
But some things don't change
Like the Hy-Vee coffee gang
And the itty bitty
Pancake City
And Edna Campbells book store
Loaded with gifts from ceiling to floor
Pagliai's Pizza is forever
Palonza? ...whatever!
There's still Thousand Hills State Park
And Truman Bulldogs with a bark
Home of the tigers too
Who knew?
Kirksville's interesting at the least
In Missouri's Great Northeast

# HOW OLD AM I?

When I was six I thought I was sixteen
I knew it all and was kind of mean
But then I turned forty and felt twenty-eight
A disillusioned mental state


# WHEN I WAS YOUR AGE

When I was your age...
You turned the page
We only had books
Stove tops for cooks
No computer devices
Stickers with prices
No cell phone
No touch tone
A quarter to call
Seems so small
Money from a machine
Remained to be seen
Brushing teeth once a day was fine
Instead of 8, noon and 9
Riding in truck beds was fun
Legal for everyone
Seat belts, what are they?
Not used in the day
Students followed rules
No security in schools
"Green" meant money
Tails were funny
Cinnamon toothpicks
No Netflix
Slower maturity
No airport security
Played outside
Most food was fried
From yesterday to today
We've come a long way
Many second chances
Lots of advances
Though not all grand or planned
Someday you'll understand

## SISTERS BEFORE MISTERS

Before I had a mister
I had a sister
Thankfully she's still around
Just wish we lived in the same big town
She's the best mom
Remains calm
Keeps things tidy
Can be rather mighty
Has a good ear
Will drink a beer
I love her chocolate cake
And that she's never ever fake
She's my very best friend
Love her 'til the end
But I must shout out some cheers
She's older by five years!

# MISS WARD

That principal, Ms. Ward
She's never bored
Always busy
In a tizzy
Running a school
She's no fool
Making sure kids learn
And take their turn
High fives
Nine lives
Pep talks
Little walks
Well dressed
Rarely stressed
She cares about us
And waits by the bus
She gives us that look
With her eyebrow hook
And on the intercom
She's the bomb
On a personal note
She can't drive a boat
To bed by ten
A really good friend
She eats no meat
And nothing sweet
She's an exercise fanatic
And a little dramatic
But the very best part
Is her loving heart

# PENELOPE

Little Miss Penelope
Did not follow the recipe
She used an inch
Instead of a pinch
And one whole cup
Of Heinz Ketch-up
Brown sugar instead of salt
A whole lot of chocolate malt
A stick of peppered beef jerky
A piece of Thanksgiving turkey
Jelly beans
And collard greens
Birthday cake
And barbecued steak
Tater tots
And pretzel knots
An orangesicle dream
A can of whipped cream
Chocolate covered cherries
Peaches and berries
An once of soda pop
A mint cough drop
A baked potato that's cheesy
An egg over-easy
A final splash of root beer
Candy sprinkles for cheer
She was proud of her concoction
So she tried to sell it at an auction
Many came to see
This food potpourri
But not a single bid
For this culinary kid

# PETER STEAK EATER

Little boy Peter
A tiny Steak Eater
Veggies are a battle
But he loves the cattle
The redder
The better
Medium rare
He won't share
Juices dripping
Used for dipping
Bread and such
Can't get too much

# PLAIN GRILLED CHEESE PLEASE

Please don't sneeze
On my grilled cheese
For I like it plain
Without rain

# NATURE'S CANDY

Natures Candy
It's so dandy!
Naturally sweet
Such a treat!
A plum, a pear
A banana to share
Lemons and limes
Good every time
A big strawberry
Kiwi that's hairy
Pineapple chunks
Much better than junk
Apples diced
Oranges sliced
Ripe bing cherries
And big blueberries
Honeydew
Watermelon, too
Nature's candy
It's so dandy

## FRIED CHICKEN

a bucket o' chicken
it's finger lickin'
fried to perfection
there is no objection
ummmmmm good
understood
a wing, a thigh
a breast to try
I pick
drumstick
ummmmm yum

# WHAT AM I?

I'm fun to slurp
And will make you burp
I like to make loops
I'm good in soups
I'm sometimes thick, sometimes thin
I like to hang from your chin
I'm found in a bowl or on a plate
I'm a carbohydrate
What am I?

## FAVORITE MUNCHIE

Chips are my favorite munchie
Because they are oh so crunchy
BBQ or plain
Yummy food for me brain
Crunch crunch crunch
Good with lunch
Crunch crunch crunch
Feeds a bunch
Crunch crunch crunch
Fun to munch!

## TATER TOT CASSEROLE

Casserole
In a bowl
Lots of cheese
It's a breeze
Tater tots
Served real hot
Everyone likes
Even tikes


## BOWELS THAT GROWL

I really must need food
Because my tummy's in a mood
It gurgles and growls
Or is that my bowels?

# 8 OUNCE CAN

It's hard to be a man
With an 8 oz can
No tall boy
Just a decoy
The 12 ouncer's baby
Little sister, maybe
One for you
That will do
Three for me
I have to pee

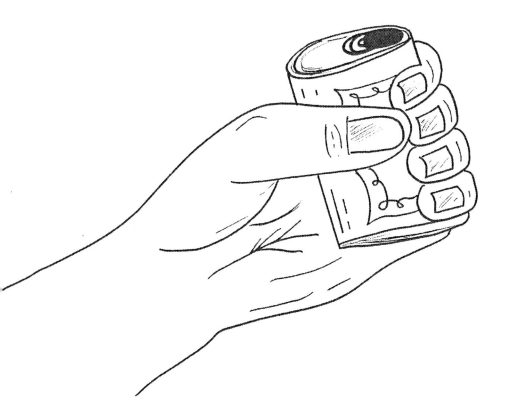

## LICK

I might be sick
Because I like to lick
Not just food
But whatever's my mood
Bottoms of shoes
Bottles of glue
The grocery cart
My lego parts
My stuffed cat
The bathtub mat
My spending money
The Easter bunny
Is this a curse?
It could be worse
I could first pick
Then lick

# SLURP AND BURP, BURP AND SLURP

Things I like to do
There are two
Slurp and burp
Burp and slurp
Better than a toy
When you're a boy
Who enjoys
Making noise
Slurp and burp
Burp and slurp


# SCAB PICKER

While sleeping at night
I feel it pull tight
It's crusty and hard
A little scarred
It's starting to heal
In time for a meal
Scab picker
Nothing sicker

# CHARLIE AND KATE

Charlie is a dog version of Kate
So excited and can never wait
They are both at an adolescent stage
Sharing the exact same age
Neither can settle down
Their eyes...a beautiful brown
They would say "yes" to hypoallergenic
And "no" to the doctor's so so clinic
They both have great hair
Neither likes to share
Both play with toys
Both make noise
Both jump high
Both cry
Both are slim
Both swim
Steal food? They just might
Both have an appetite
And at the end of the day
I have to say
There's no dispute
The dog version of Kate is cute

## OLIVER, THE PUG

Oliver, the pug
Has his own rug
He can't help but snort
And he's rather short
He climbs his stairs
To a bed he shares
With his master
His heart beats faster
He loves her so much
Her doggie touch
She gives him treats
He eats and eats
And runs around
He's very wound
He gives a good hug
Oliver, the pug

# GLOW HUNT

I was the leader
At Big Cedar
I had to be blunt
At Glow Hunt
The team was quite a mix
Ages five to sixty-six
With a small flashlight
Searching at night
Walking miles
Keeping smiles
Lots of thrills
Up hills
Through water
We got hotter
Feeling it burn
Made a wrong turn
We had fears, tears and cheers

Lots of glowing souvenirs
Back on track
Filled the sack
With eight glow toys
Let's make some noise
Whoot! Whoot!
Hoot! Hoot!
We're feeling good
Like Robin Hood
We got this race
We kept the pace
But wait, we're missing two!
What will we do?
To the finish line we run
We think we've won
Turns out we're not fast
Got second to last

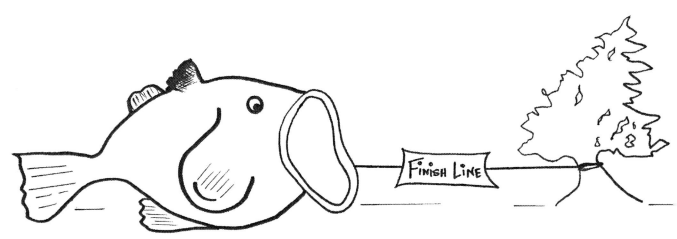

## ARNIE'S BARN TOOTH FAIRY

I was eating a taco and drinking my juice
When suddenly I realized my tooth was loose
And with little doubt
I pulled it out
Now there were three
Missing from me
I felt a little tingle
And heard a little jingle
There was something in the air
A glimmer and a flare
No more thoughts about it, not 'til the bill arrived
Dad was speechless and had to be revived
We couldn't believe our eyes
What a surprise
I was so happy inside
I smiled with pride
A dollar bill and a special note
Here's what she wrote....

# TODAY

Today Today Today
Tomorrow and yesterday
Love this show
Here's what you should know
It's more than one hour
Of hottie Matt Lauer
All the latest fashion
But news is their passion
Covering the Royal Palace
With Natalie Morales
And Al Roker
He's a joker
But he's got it altogether
When telling the weather
They're all pretty and witty
In New York City
There's lots of laughs
Mind-numbing crafts
News News News
And music too
Kathie Lee and Hoda know how to work a crowd
I find myself laughing out loud
And I'd like to go on a shopping spree
With Miss Savannah Guthrie
She welcomed baby Vale on August 13
The prettiest baby you've ever seen
And, oh, how I wish I had her seat
I'd make the show complete
In Studio 1A
Today Today Today

## SIMPLE PIMPLE

Why can't a pimple
Just be simple?
It invades my space
Takes over my face
OOOOOOOoooooooozes
GOOOOOoooooooozes
WOOOOOoooooooozes
Spots
Dots
Knots
Each stands alone
On a tiny throne
Below my lower lip
On my nose tip
Or on my chin
Pimple...you win!

# STINKY STINK

There's things that stink
Like bad breath and printing ink
A stinky stink
Don't ya think?
And other things that don't smell
But stink as well
Like cavities
And skinned up knees
A bee sting
And static cling
Booster shots
And tiny knots
Being grounded
Being hounded
Long lines
Traffic fines
Tattle tales
Chipped nails
Mosquito bites
Delayed flights
All stinky things indeed
But I think it's agreed
The stinkiest of the stink
Skunks, I think

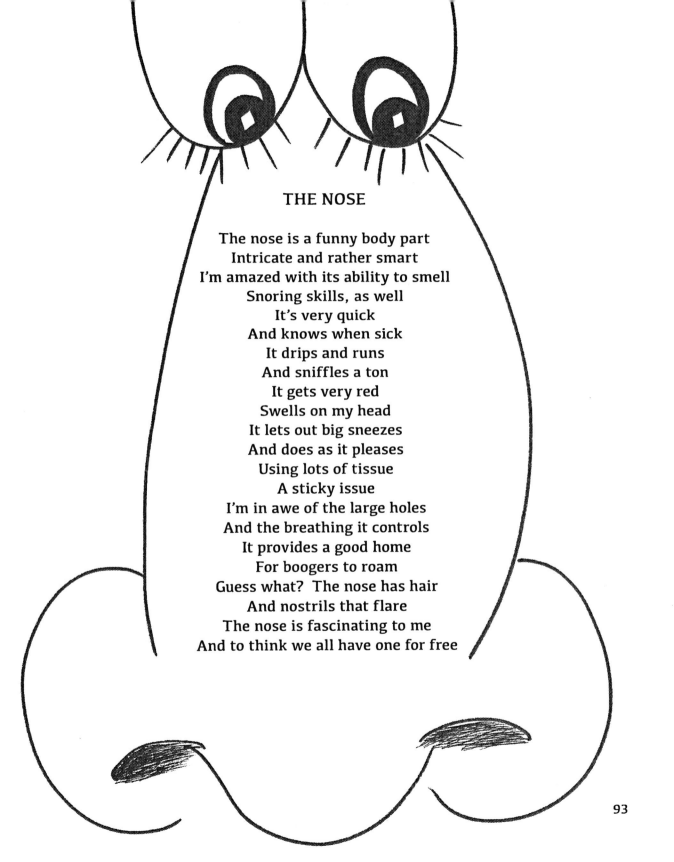

## THE NOSE

The nose is a funny body part
Intricate and rather smart
I'm amazed with its ability to smell
Snoring skills, as well
It's very quick
And knows when sick
It drips and runs
And sniffles a ton
It gets very red
Swells on my head
It lets out big sneezes
And does as it pleases
Using lots of tissue
A sticky issue
I'm in awe of the large holes
And the breathing it controls
It provides a good home
For boogers to roam
Guess what?  The nose has hair
And nostrils that flare
The nose is fascinating to me
And to think we all have one for free

## PLAY DOUGH

Uh Oh
Play Dough
Make a baby
Don't mean maybe
Pull and roll
Damage control
Shape and mold
Make it hold
Arms and legs
Looks like pegs
Nose and eyes
In disguise
Uh Oh
No one will know
A baby it is
Not Cheez Whiz

## UNCLE MATT

He has a cat
His name is Matt
Dad's younger brother
Has the same mother
I'm sure he has a history
But he remains a mystery

## SIPPY CUP HICCUPS

When I drink from sippy cups
I get the hiccups
I went to see Dr. Rupp
Who diagnosed sippy cup hiccups

## SNUGGLE ME OR ELSE

The snuggle bug
Requires a hug
A big squeeze
Pretty please
If no embrace
Sad face
And an endless supply
Of a whiny cry
So when asked to snuggle
Don't make it a struggle
Go get your hugs
Or buy ear plugs

## ALMOST RIGHT

I don't always say things right
Just like the other night...
I said,
"A cooker is what I want to be
When I growed up to twenty-three"
When asked about school that day
I said, "play...
and Mrs. Hirsch teached reading
Joe's nose was bleeding
and I digged for bugs
and finded slugs
and I keeped it in my lunchbox
and didn't telled Mrs. Knox
worser it could get
when I bited something wet
I barfed my PBJ
and throwed it away"
I don't always get things right
But I thinked I'm pretty bright

# PETUNIA P. POCKET MOUSE

She lives in a pocket, not a house
Petunia P. is a pocket mouse
She has a fast heart rate
And stays up late
She doesn't like my cat
And won't lie flat
I know this to be true
Oh yes I do
Because Petunia P. Pocket Mouse is *my* pocket mouse
She lives in the pocket of my polka-dotted blouse

## SCOUT MOM

I'm a Scout mom
I must stay calm
It's sometimes hard
When caught off guard
But the joy of them learning
And the badges they're earning
Make it all worthwhile
I just have to smile
And to think that I played a tiny part
In shaping their beautiful hearts

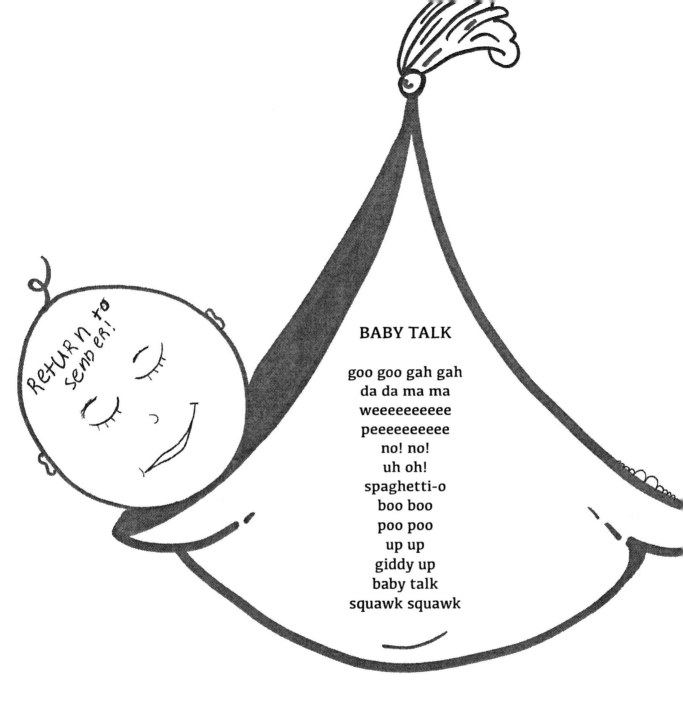

BABY TALK

goo goo gah gah
da da ma ma
weeeeeeeeee
peeeeeeeeee
no! no!
uh oh!
spaghetti-o
boo boo
poo poo
up up
giddy up
baby talk
squawk squawk

## OH BROTHER

My world was rocked
I was shocked
I'd heard the tale
It comes by mail
What a mess
The wrong address
But, Mom and dad…
They sure seem glad
As for me…
I disagree
Who's he?
It can't be
I wanted a puppy
Or even a guppy
I know the fix
Because I'm six
When all are in bed
I'll write on his head
"Return to Sender"
I won't surrender!

# DAD THINGS

There are things about dad
That are totally rad
His whiskers for one
The fact that he's fun
His cowboy boots
His stinky toots
His electrical wire
He cooks with fire
His white truck
His good luck
His computer skills
His cholesterol pills
His collection of tools
My dad rules


# WHEN DAD AND I SHOP

I really like to shop
In a pretty dress and flip flops
But Dad would rather eat a bug
Then have to shop for a rug
But when we go to the hardware store
We have a bond you can't ignore
We go on candy shopping sprees
All made by Hershey's
But don't tell my mom
She won't stay calm
And it's not because my teeth might rot
But because the lightbulbs we forgot

# DAD'S LIST

**Mom has something for dad**
**It's on a notepad**
**It's a loooooooooooooooooooooonnnnnnnnnnnnng list**
**And goes like this…**

Honey, I love you
Honey, please do
Before I return
Don't crash and turn
Shake out the rugs
Spray for bugs
Call the sitter
Clean the litter
Fill cars with gas
Take out trash
Vacuum stairs
Sink repairs
Change sheets
Classroom treats (1st grade- Mrs. Kinney)
Trim the trees
Find the keys
Make a casserole
Clean the toilet bowl
Mow the yard
I know it's hard
This list of chores
It's all yours
Honey, thank you for working like Mad
Tomorrow's Honey Do won't be so bad.
XO XO ♡ MOM

# KATE AT THE PLATE

When I'm 6 and playing baseball
All the world becomes so small
It's the size of first base
Or that throw in the face
It's the size of a strike
Or a pitch I don't like
It's the size of a slide
Which hurts my hide
It's the size of sweat
From my helmet
But when I finally make contact with the ball
The world's no longer so small
It becomes larger than large
I can feel the charge
My face feels the breeze
I touch first with ease
I can hear the cheering crowd
Mom and dad are proud

# OUR GIRL

Our girl
She loves to twirl
She's kind & smart
She dances with heart
We want you to know
We love her so!

# PHOTOGRAPHER

You'll find her at a photo shoot
She's funny and she's rather cute
She talks about gas
To make kids laugh
Stinky feet and boogers too
But if that won't do…
She bribes with candy
It's always handy
She wants them to stop wiggling
But prefers that they're giggling
She has a bag of tricks
And oh, her baby pics!
They are the best
Newborns at rest
And how she can make them bend
The babies really are her friends
She captures that smile
With such great style
Lissy Early, memory maker
Lissy Early, picture taker

## PICK ONE

It's fun
Stripes or plaid
Mom or dad
Boxers or Briefs
Royals or Chiefs
Funny or scholastic
Paper or plastic
Learn or teach
Mountains or beach
Listen or talk
Ride or walk
Small or large
Cash or charge
Drive or fly
Bake or fry
Cat or dog
Tweet or blog
Spring or fall
Short or tall
Rain or snow
Gotta go!

# REALLY?

Airplane hog
Sawing a log
Needs a bigger place
He's in my space
A human Hank
A really large tank
Extra wide width
Stinky sandwich
Rustling his papers
Smells like capers
Coffee spill
Sit still
Ahhhh chooing
And spewing
Probably chewing
His Arm in my side
I want to hide
Hit me again
I'll pinch your chin
What to do
Pew!!!!
Need a fan
An exit plan
A Black and Tan
A puking can
Should be Jacquie
Please just smack me!

## CRAIG'S DESK

My name's Craig
And I've been plagued
With a messy desk
It's grotesque
Stains and drips
From coffee sips
Shoes with mud
Paper cut blood
My trash can reeks
It's been two weeks
Since it was taken out
I ate trout
And sauerkraut
I like my mess
On my desk
it's grotesque

## SPLAT!

Headed to Mr. Sneed's
At highway speeds
Splat!
What was that?

## MINIVAN MAN

I'm a minivan man
With a great tan
With seating for eight
And a personalized plate
A sliding door
Need I say more?
I think not!
I look hot!
Cruising through town
With my windows down
Air is flowing
Hair is blowing
Tunes blaring
Women staring
I practice visualization
But then... a realization
Passed on the left
By a Corvette

## GIFT OF DREAMS

Beautiful child, what do you see in your dreams?
Fairies and castles with flowing streams?
Do you hop as fast as a bunny?
Stop to watch the bees make honey?
Are you among flowers?
In rain showers?
Or are you flying high on a unicorn
Admiring his single horn?
Are the birds singing your favorite song?
Do the animals invite you to come along
On a walk in the woods
Where everything is good?
There is no fear
All's sincere
This place is for you
It can be true
It will change with the days
Never seizing to amaze
It never dies
For all to realize

# MYSTERY CAN

I'm the man
With the mystery can
Guess what's inside
I've nothing to hide
I'll give you a clue
Let's see how you do
From **A** to **Z**
Turn the page to see

**A**
Outer space
My favorite place

**B**
Under your shirt
Collects dirt

**C**
Knows the time
Likes to chime

**D**
Doesn't meow
But goes bow wow

**E**
Stairs that go up and down
Helps people move around

**F**
A love that can't be measured
Someone treasured

**G**
Where things grow
Vegetables to sow

**H**
A type of squeeze
Guaranteed to please

**I**
On the desk in the den
In a ball point pen

**J**
Orange, Grape, and Apple
How 'bout a Snapple?

**K**
Unlocks diaries and doors
Cars and more

**L**
Used to kiss
Your baby sis

**M**
Keep it handy
To purchase candy

**N**
I have heads and tails
I'm five at all sales

**O**
There's no dispute
I'm a color and a fruit

**P**
A type of bear
With black and white hair

**Q**
A small test
Do your best

**R**
Cockadoodledoo
Guess who?

**S**
Turkey and cheese
Mayo please

**T**
Where the dog begs
I have four legs

**U**
Change before bed
Don't wear on your head

**V**
Long and blue
Blood runs through

**W**
Nothing compares
To facial hairs

**X**
Pictures of bones
But not kidney stones

**Y**
I'm yellow and with a dozen
Of my first cousins

**Z**
Home of kangaroos
Tigers and monkeys too

| | |
|---|---|
| **A** ASTRONAUT | **N** NICKEL |
| **B** BELLY BUTTON | **O** ORANGE |
| **C** CLOCK | **P** PANDA |
| **D** DOG | **Q** QUIZ |
| **E** ESCALATOR | **R** ROOSTER |
| **F** FRIEND | **S** SANDWICH |
| **G** GARDEN | **T** TABLE |
| **H** HUG | **U** UNDERWEAR |
| **I** INK | **V** VEIN |
| **J** JUICE | **W** WHISKERS |
| **K** KEY | **X** X-RAYS |
| **L** LIPS | **Y** YOLK |
| **M** MONEY | **Z** ZOO |

## AC

It's a little confusing to me
This thing called an AC
In the window it sits
Cold air it spits
It's one big box
It rumbles and rocks
But it does its task
We don't even ask
By blowing cold air
Here and there
It's kind of like ice
And I thought it nice
To give honorable mention
For this loud invention

## CAT SCRATCH FEVER

There's no twist
Cat Scratch Fever really does exist
But you can avoid that
By being nice to your cat

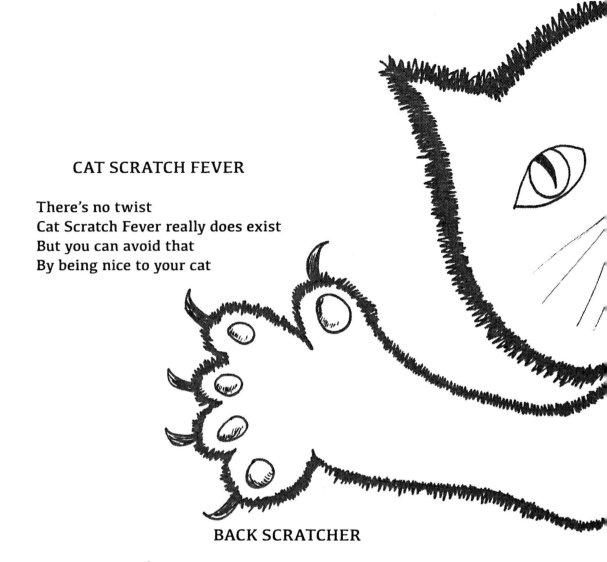

## BACK SCRATCHER

If only there was a switch
To turn off my tickle itch
It's on my back up high
Scratch, Scratch, I try
Scratch, Scratch, a little more
I itch to my core
Scratch, Scratch, but I can't reach
"Scratch my back!" I screech
And finally her small hand comes over
"Ahhhhh... higher, higher, no lower"
You know what I mean?
Everyone needs a back scratching machine

## IMPERFECT IS PERFECT

Imperfect to me, is perfect to me
Perfect I will never be
I don't even try
And here's why
There's mishaps and mistakes
Many things at stake
Misunderstandings
Mishandlings
Miscalculations
Misconfigurations
Not all words rhyme
All the time
But you do your best
And forget the rest
Imperfect is perfect to me
Perfect I will never be

Thank you, Kate, for showing me the world through your beautiful brown eyes. Your creative spirit shines in Petunia P. Pocket Mouse and Mermaid Sister. And to my husband, Sam, thank you for loving my brain that never shuts off and for holding my dreams close to your own heart.

# ALPHABETICAL INDEX

8 Ounce Can, 83

AC, 117
Almost Right, 97
Always There, 21
Arm Pits, 43
Arnie's Barn Tooth Fairy, 89
Awake, 23

Baby Talk, 100
Back Scratcher, 118
Bathroom Words, 13
Bear Hunt, 4
Birthday Suit, 29
Bossy Rossy, 30-31
Bowels that Growl, 82
Bully Bill, 33
Busy Bus, 62-63

Cartoons, 47
Cat Scratch Fever, 118
Charlie and Kate, 86
Clip and Snip, 53
Collection, 26
Craig's Desk, 110

Dad Things, 102
Dad's List, 103
Date, 66

Elfis, 41
Empty, 35

Face Cleaner, 15
Father Bruce, 64
Favorite Munchie, 81
Footsteps, 67
Fried Chicken, 80

Garbage Can Man, 55
Getting Dressed, 52
Gift of Dreams, 114
Gotta Go, 10
Glow Hunt, 88
Grandma, 60
Great Grandpa, 59
Growing Up Kirksville, 69

High Low, 61
How Old Am I?, 70
Homework, 50

I Love My Mom, 18
I Love You, 17
Imperfect is Perfect, 119

Kate at the Plate, 104

Lemonade Stand, 39
Let it Bee, 5
Lick, 84
Life *101*, 57
Lunchbox Thief, 45
Magic in a Bar, 14
Mermaid Sister, 37

Milk Fountain, 44
Minivan Man, 113
Miss Erin and Miss Kay, 65
Miss Ward, 72
Mixed Veggie Wedgies, 9
Mommies are the Best, 16
My Chester Raccoon, 19
Mystery Can, 115-116

Nature's Candy, 78
Nest, 60
Night Time Cover Thief, 28
The Nose, 93
No Use, 35

Oh Brother, 101
Oliver, the Pug, 87
One Man Wrecking Machine, 3
Our Girl, 105
Our Ugly Toes, 7

Penelope, 74
Perfect Study Buddy, 51
Peter Steak Eater, 76
Petunia P. Pocket Mouse, 98
Photographer, 107
Pick One, 108
Plain Grilled Cheese Please, 77
Play Dough, 94
Pop UP, 46
Problem Solver, 32

Really?, 109
Red, 34

Scab Picker, 85
Scout Mom, 99
Silence, 27
Simple Pimple, 91
Sippy Cup Hiccups, 95
Sisters Before Misters, 71
Slurp and Burp, Burp and Slurp, 85
Smoocharoo, 20
Snipe Hunt, 6
Snuggle Me or Else, 96
Splat!, 112
Spoon, 22
Spring Break, 48
Stinky Stink, 92
Sugary Boogery Book, 1

Talk Talk Talker, 56
Tater Tot Casserole, 82
Tattoo, 42
Today, 90
True Love, 58

Uncle Matt, 95

What Am I?, 81
When I Was Your Age, 70
When Dad and I Shop, 102
Where Am I?, 49
Where is Papa?, 11
Wired, 25

# SUGAR BOOGER INDEX

**All SUGAR, no booger ...** super sweet
and really neat

AC, 117
Almost Right, 97
Always There, 21
Arnie's Barn Tooth Fairy, 89
Awake, 23

Baby Talk, 100
Back Scratcher, 118
Bear Hunt, 4
Bowels that Growl, 82
Busy Bus, 62-63

Cartoons, 47
Cat Scratch Fever, 118
Charlie and Kate, 86

Dad Things, 102
Dad's List, 103
Date, 66

Elfis, 41

Face Cleaner, 15
Father Bruce, 64
Favorite Munchie, 81
Footsteps, 67
Fried Chicken, 80

Getting Dressed, 52
Gift of Dreams, 114
Glow Hunt, 88
Grandma, 60
Great Grandpa, 59
Growing Up Kirksville, 69

High Low, 61
How Old Am I?, 70
Homework, 50

I Love My Mom, 18
I Love You, 17
Imperfect is Perfect, 119

Kate at the Plate, 104

Lemonade Stand, 39
Let it Bee, 5
Life *101*, 57
Lunchbox Thief, 45

Magic in a Bar, 14
Mermaid Sister, 37
Milk Fountain, 44
Minivan Man, 113
Miss Erin and Miss Kay, 65
Miss Ward, 72
Mommies are the Best, 16
My Chester Raccoon, 19
Mystery Can, 115-116

Nature's Candy, 78
Nest, 60
Night Time Cover Thief, 28

Oh Brother, 101
Oliver, the Pug, 87
One Man Wrecking Machine, 3
Our Girl, 105
Our Ugly Toes, 7

Penelope, 74
Perfect Study Buddy, 51
Peter Steak Eater, 76
Petunia P. Pocket Mouse, 98
Photographer, 107
Pick One, 108
Plain Grilled Cheese Please, 77
Play Dough, 94
Pop UP, 46

Scout Mom, 99
Silence, 27
Sippy Cup Hiccups, 95
Sisters Before Misters, 71
Smoocharoo, 20
Snipe Hunt, 6
Snuggle Me or Else, 96
Splat!, 112
Spring Break, 48
Sugary Boogery Book, 1

Talk Talk Talker, 56
Tater Tot Casserole, 82
Today, 90

True Love, 58

Uncle Matt, 95

What Am I?, 81
When I Was Your Age, 70
When Dad and I Shop, 102
Where Am I?, 49
Wired, 25

**Some SUGAR, Some BOOGER...** a
healthy dose of sweet and gross

8 Once Can, 83

Arm Pits, 43

Birthday Suit, 29
Bossy Rossy, 30-31
Bully Bill, 33

Clip and Snip, 53
Collection, 26
Craig's Desk, 110

Empty, 35

Garbage Can Man, 55
Gotta Go, 10

Mixed Veggie Wedgies, 9

The Nose, 93
No Use, 35

Problem Solver, 32

Really?, 109
Red, 34

Simple Pimple, 91
Slurp and Burp, Burp and Slurp, 85
Spoon, 22
Stinky Stink, 92

Tattoo, 42

Where is Papa?, 11

**All BOOGER, no sugar...** read if you
  dare, grandma beware

Bathroom Words, 13

Lick, 84

Scab Picker, 85